THE ORACLE OF BIRDS

SHORT STORIES FOR THE FIRESIDE

DONNA FAULKNER NÉE MILLER

Cover design by Donna Faulkner née Miller.

Published by Written Tales.

CONTENTS

To my Dad, Don Miller & for my family.

Familia supra omnia

INTRODUCTION

Welcome to "The Oracle of Birds: Short Stories for the Fireside," a collection of enchanting tales and poems by Donna Faulkner née Miller. In these stories, dreams, myths, and superstition come together to explore how everything is connected. Donna moves us on a journey through nature, landscapes, traditions, and cultures. Each short story and poem explores the importance of place and purpose.

This collection invites you to discover her storytelling magic. From the poem "Saturation" to "The Devil's Kiss," each piece offers a unique adventure. These tales will transport you to worlds where dreams and myths unfold. Her words create more than just a collection—it's a friendly companion for fireside reflections, urging you to explore imagination and the mysteries of the human experience.

1
SATURATION

sky knocks on parched ground,
let me in. You need my tears
and I need to weep.

HERE IS THE POEM

that unfurled
an inkling
from bayleaf
slumber.

Fractured
dreams
bridging
the netherworld

This comma,
paused
while I chewed
on my pen.

Nursed by sweet tea
this entire stanza
was
an afterthought.

I scribble
in flux,
plucking a stray hair
from my writing.

A surgeon's
scalpel
in an amateur's
grip.

Kicking rocks
by the river,
This is the poem
that insisted.

Wayfinder vines
ruminating
a conversation -
overheard.

Here is the poem
to scaffold my wilding.
Inevitable, the flourish
of weeds.

An immigrant
from old scribblings.
soliloquise is trying
to assimilate here,

I cannot tell you
where I end
and the poem begins.
All I can do is show you.

3
THE RAG DOLL RIDER

I COULDN'T HAVE CALLED for help. There had never been a phone booth on this particular street, but yet I'd vividly remembered one. Imagined I was standing beside a big red booth just as the accident had unfolded. My memory has been corrupted over the years. Infected by the emotion in that moment.

Maybe I thought I should have done something useful, as children often do, but help had come regardless. Residents had heard the bang and came scrambling from their houses.

Soon after that, we moved towns, later immigrating to New Zealand.

Decades later, I returned to that exact spot. Pulled off the scab. Stood there on the pavement remembering that hot day in summer back when I was six.

It was the summer holidays and we were sent out to 'play'. I can hear the bike coming before I see it. Hear the loud roar as it accelerates. It flies over the crest of the hill, brakes burning. The parked car, mounted. The rider flung like a ragdoll. The rag doll lay still on the road.

I smelled the burn of rubber. Stood frozen watching the cacophony unfold. A flurry of activity. Frantic people trying to do something. Save someone. Then the ambulance came.

Solemn and with care they placed the rider on the stretcher and pulled the sheet up over his face. My sister explained that he was 'gone.'

When my dad buys himself a motorbike I relive this memory, breathing in the freshly burned rubber. I recall the rag doll rider motionless, his limbs splayed on the cold road.

I calm the palpitations in my chest just enough to force a smile. Dad's joy is obvious and contagious, and so for a moment I repress my fear of bikes and death. But I still don't 'get' it. I only ride a few times with him, and just around the block.

I learned later that my Dad had owned bikes before he met Mum. But he sold his bikes when he had kids and made a promise to mum that he'd wait until the kids were older before he'd ride again.

We were older now, with kids of our own. So Dad brought a new fridge freezer, top of the range, to pacify mum. Then he bought himself a superbike. He would explain to me in great detail all the things that mattered, I remember only that it had six cylinders.

Mum tried to go along with it, got on board, sat on the back. They set off on a trip right around New Zealand. Mum didn't enjoy it, her back ached so she took a plane home. Dad carried on riding, and finished his tour. Three years later he was dead. He wasn't killed on his bike, his big heart gave out when he was fifty two.

I met my husband Victor ten years later. He drives trucks for a living and lives in one too. A vintage house truck. He woos me over bread, becoming a regular at the bakery where I work. Later he tells me that he had rode and owned Harley's and triumphs for years. Circumstances had forced their sale but he had a longing to ride that lingered.

When my kids were all but grown Victor brought a Harley Davidson. A wide glide, in red. Red is my favourite colour. He said it was our time now and he missed riding so much. I wasn't at all interested.

I told him the story of the rag doll rider but he was still determined to persuade me. He was sure once I tried it, I'd love it. I couldn't understand what all the fuss was about. Traveling all bundled up and exposed to the elements. So I put it off for as long as possible.

Vic customized the Harley to tempt me. He had a bigger seat made, a sissy bar installed. Then he brought me my own riding jacket and pants. Weeks passed, and he continued to ride solo but he desperately wanted me to share in the experience, and eventually I ran out of plausible excuses. It was time to try.

It was a fine Saturday. He stood at the door waiting in his helmet and his gloves. I took my time getting ready. Delay tactics. I went through rituals too. Brushed my teeth, twice. Placed a moonstone rock in my jacket pocket.

My thoughts returned again to the mangled limbs of the rag doll rider and I couldn't convince my jelly legs to walk out the door.

Victor waited without saying much but I could feel his impatience. Determined to make an attempt, I had a surprise revelation, listening to music might help calm me. I jammed my headphones in my helmet, the wires were annoying but I persevered.

I'm surprised that he could breathe as we rode that first ride together, my interlocked hands strangling his waist. I thought of nothing, but listened to my playlist. The next song. Then the next, and I thought of my Dad.

I think of Dad often when we are out on the bike. There are no barriers to this connection. Sharing the same sights he would have seen. We become the scenery, the cold breath of snow through the alpine Pass.

We've had 'our' bike for four years now. We do trips around the South Island on big red.

My helmet has been upgraded, there's built-in sunglasses and my music bluetooths from my phone. I have over ten hours of songs on Spotify. I often sing along.

We rode eight hours to Invercargill. For the last four hours it continuously rained. Rogue rain sneaked inside my collar and snaked its way down my neck. I had to peel my soaked pants off on arrival and my socks squelched puddles in boots.

There's been the inevitable near misses, and we've had a car almost hit us at the lights. I tell myself that it's all a part of the adventure. We pull over and have a coffee and ride on.

I still think of the rag doll rider. Mainly when I feel the bike break suddenly or the side wind seems determined to push me off. I think of my Dad even more. Remember his smile when he told me about his superbike with six cylinders.

I stopped locking my fingers around Victor's torso. I rest my hands upon my knees now instead.

We have a favorite corner, a long sweeper on the road out of town. We yolk together and lean low, riding the corner like a rail.

4
RIDING MOUNTAINS

Riders yoke,
two wheels
coil corners

snaking
the narrow pass
beneath.

Alpine crests
levitate
the looming haze

Frustrated
behind a camper
gears let out a sigh.

Tourists overtaken,
the road ahead
now clear.

Mountains ascend,
the bend
a tight caress.

Valleys applaud
the engines
thrum.

Skirting roadsides
waving lupins
painted purple.

Riders taste
sweet
blossom's breath.

5
THE MENACE IN THE MANSION

ANDY ARCHED his eyebrow at the clump of dirt out of place. It wasn't there this morning when his girlfriend left for work. Nor this afternoon when he'd polished the kitchen faucets to a mirror's shine. But without explanation, there it was. A clump of dirt sabotaging appearances from deep within luxurious piles of thick carpet.

"This is why I was right to have fired Sylvia yesterday," he lied.

"Clearly, she'd never cleaned up properly."

But in truth, Andy's girlfriend had seeded the idea to fire old Sylvia. She'd rolled her eyes whenever Sylvia was there cleaning. She'd blatantly mocked the old woman as she'd gone about her duties, singing to herself. She laughed at Sylvia's old black skirt, which hung over her ample backside, trailing like a tarpaulin.

"Why can't you get a real cleaner, someone ...younger, and why is she always clasping that old feather duster, you know she brings it with her every day?"

It's true Sylvia had made even Andy cringe on the rare occasion that she was still there when Andy had arrived home early with company.

Yesterday a few colleagues had accompanied Andy home after lunch for a celebratory tipple, a big client secured. Sylvia had been bumped into by a couple of inebriated guests larking about, and had broken a vase with a swing of her ample hips.The room stood still at the commotion. The vase shattering. It was the last straw.

Andy had already had a bit to drink by then and encouraged by his smirking girlfriend, he had overreacted. He'd shouted at Sylvia , humiliating her infront of his guests,

"I asked for a housekeeper and all I got was an old Menace! I'm sorry Sylvia, this isn't working" He yelled.

He knew the broken vase wasn't Sylvia's fault and that the old woman really needed this job. But he suppressed any sense of compassion and fairness, this was just the excuse he needed to appease his girlfriend.

Sylvia quickly offered her apologies and tried to sweep up the broken vase but Andy wouldn't hear of it. He began bundling the old woman up, corralling her towards the door.

"Pack up your things, you are done here!"

He quickly crammed some cash into Sylvia's calloused hands, gesturing toward the door with a casual malice.

The room fell silent. Andy tried to turn his back, and carry on his conversation with one of his guests, but Sylvia locked him in a stare and held him there. Her mouth opened to speak,

" You are a vile man, but I'll give you a menace!"

Her smile widened as she paused to laugh. He couldn't shift his focus and he fixated on her last remaining teeth.

"All the work I've ever done here will be undone, and it will *haunt* you"

She deliberately eyeballed each individual in the room. They all stood dumbfounded, champagne poised in crystal flutes, their mouths wide open.

Sylvia picked up her duster and as she got to the front door she stood in the entrance. Her stance wide, Muttering something that sounded like a curse.

She lassoed her duster with three big sweeps in the air and shook it out on the welcome mat. Then turned and left without another word, slamming the door behind her.

It had been rather dramatic, igniting quite the excitement after Sylvia departed.

"Bravo, bravo" the room erupted into applause and laughter.

"That was quite the display Andy" someone laughed.

Andy had been on the phone to the agency first thing that morning. He needed to secure a replacement cleaner, and quickly. Meanwhile, there was this fresh spot of dirt at the entranceway, and it was bothering him.

Andy was a stickler for appearances, and a dirty house simply would not do. He bent down to pick it up but the dirt was stubborn and wouldn't budge. It was stuck like chewing gum in matted hair. He tutted.

He would not tolerate rogue fly corpses on windowsills. He did not entertain living plants with their falling foliage. There were no paw prints smudging glass doors here nor cat fur on the furniture. He was proud of his sprawling house. Orderly and clean. There was no place here for dust and dirt, not ever!

Annoyed, he rushed off and returned with the vacuum cleaner. Pushing the head repeatedly,scrubbing over the same spot. He checked every two or three sweeps to see if the dirt had gone. But each time he looked, the spot of dirt was actually bigger.

How could that be? he thought. He stopped vacuuming and rubbed his chin quite puzzled.

The dirty spot wasn't spreading out like a fresh spill or stain, but it was growing. It began to scaffold itself upwards. With an animated static, it quickly commandeered vertical space.Within minutes, the dirt became an intricate web of filthy threads seeking form.

He watched in disbelief at the dirt in its speedy evolution. Self assembling threads created legs, and the thing stood up. Weaving itself a massive torso, then a rudimentary face. Humming a tune like a snake charmer's flute, the dirty Menace appeared to be beckoning something.

Legions of dust and dirt emerged from their hiding spots. From corners and behind cupboards, dirt became tumbleweed gathering up all the dust that had ever been banished.

From beneath the couch it came too, massing together in colorful formations of thread and lint. The dust balls rolled like an avalanche towards the Menace.

Andy's skin itched furiously at the bizarre spectacle.

Cobwebs emerged from high crevices and crawled along the ceiling above his head. He scratched at himself furiously as specs of dirt dropped into his carefully combed hair. The webs slid down from the walls. Loaded with full threads of sticky mess, they too were commandeered by the Menace.

Andy staggered a little and clutched his chest in disbelief as he watched clumps of black soot abseil down the chimney. Marching in single file like an army of ants over his thickly piled carpet. They too were absorbed by the Menace.

Andy came to his senses.He promptly pulled the head off the vacuum, turned the power to full, and sucked. The exposed pipe aimed at the dirty monster.

The vacuum made a lot of noise, but it did nothing.

In a matter of moments the Menace had grown formidable. This embodiment of dirt cast a foreboding shadow in the lounge.

This had to be a nightmare. He needed to wake up. So he rubbed his eyes. But the Menace remained. When that didn't work, he slapped his own face, hard.

The Menace loomed larger.

Animated with the clumsiness of a toddler the dirty beast bent down to face Andy and mouthed.

"I am your curse."

The Menace grew visibly larger with each inhale of dust and dirt.

Petrified, Andy tried to turn his face away, the foul breath of the Menace nauseating. He stumbled backward, over-whelmed by the monstrosity before him.

He was desperate to escape. But he was trapped between the wall and the Menace.It was a most unenviable position. The vacuum cleaner remained limp and useless in his hands.

6

THE FABLE OF THE SPIDER AND THE HOUSEMATE

THE SPIDER DIDN'T KNOW her real name, but she assumed it was "Arghhh." Whenever she initiated conversations with her housemate, the housemate responded with a high-pitched "Arghhh."

"I like it in this corner," the spider said to her housemate. "I've been busy spreading silk between the corner and the wall, and look, I've already caught a blowfly and a moth," she boasted proudly.

"Arghhh," the housemate screamed and ran out of the room.

She promptly returned with a feather duster which she launched at the web, muttering about the dust and mess of cobwebs.

"Stop, stop," cried the spider from her hiding spot behind the curtain.

The housemate stretched up the feather duster, and in a twirling and twisting motion gathered up the beautiful silk creation, pulling away the trapped dinner of moths and blowflies.

"Fine," sighed the spider to her housemate despondently, "I see you don't like me making my web in the lounge. I will find another corner in which to weave my web."

The spider often watched her housemate from a distance. She watched her shoo the flies that hovered in the kitchen hunkering after the housemates' food. So she spoke to her housemate and said,

"I see flies congregating in the kitchen. I see that the warm weather and the smell of your steak cooking entices them in through your open window."

The housemate didn't respond. Maybe she hadn't heard.

"I will do you a favour and spin my web above the window to trap them for you."

The housemate spotted the spider just as soon as she had finished creating her web, and she screamed at the spider again. "Arghhh."

"Get out, get out of my house," the housemate shouted.

"I'm setting my web to catch the flies which annoy you so much in the kitchen," replied the spider.

The housemate ran off, quickly returning with a hungry vacuum cleaner. Its sucking nozzle extended up and pursued the fleeing spider. "Get out! get out of my house."

The spider could feel the air from the vacuum pulling at her legs, "Stop, stop, you are ripping my legs off."

The spider barely escaped scuttling behind the light bulb. She stayed hidden and scared for a very long time.

" It's obvious that you don't want to share space with a spider, nor do you value our shared tenancy, but worse of all I think you actually want me dead!" the spider wept.

The spider skulked across the ceiling and into the bedroom, careful to avoid the housemate.

The spider, like all house spiders, can create two types of webs and strum a third. The first web was physical, a trap for prey. This web could be remade every day. The second was invisible, a web spun with magical intent to bounce back unwanted visitors from the 'other side' . Its silk was rare and had to be preserved. House Spiders were also able to strum the web of the world. This web of creation bridged time and connected all living things.

The spider, in her sadness, decided to pack up and leave. Seeking a new home with a more welcoming housemate.

So the spider carefully deconstructed the magical web she had crafted specifically to protect the housemate in her slumber. As she left, she used her legs and little voice to strum along the web of life.

"Hear me fellow house spiders, this place is most unwelcoming to spiders. In fact, it could be quite deadly to our kind. I decree that none may spin their webs here ever again." And the spider left the house never to return.

That night, the housemate went to sleep, trying to avoid the moths that bombarded her room at night.

Not long into finally settling , she felt the room drop suddenly cold and her body fell into a terrifying state of paralysis.

Her eyes opened, and she could see that the night hag had returned. The terrifying hag sat heavy on her chest. The housemate began to panic and struggled to breathe. But the night hag had grown heavier and angrier over all these months.

"That spider and her magical web stopped my nightly visits. Now she's gone for good and I'm back," cackled the night hag.

Her putrid breath poisoned the room, and she took great pleasure in tormenting the housemate, pulling out from her mind a string of dark fears long repressed.

And with each passing day, more flies came and stayed. Making a nuance of themselves in the kitchen. Blowflies blew in every window, bouncing unhindered from wall to wall. At twilight, moths by their hundreds descended upon the unprotected house. Each night the housemate's slumber was ruined by nightmares and ghostly visitors.

The housemate soon grew sick, tired, and weary. She lamented the departure of the spider, and pleaded out loud for the spider to return.

But her pleas were futile. It was now woven into the Web of all Creation that she would never have the benefit of a spider as a housemate again.

7
ITI MANU
MOST UNFORTUNATE

Low flying, frantic flapping.
Chaos calms quickly
within a moment - mid swoop.
Whirlwinds of dusty feathers.
Melding with cracked bones.

Monday mornings birdsong
swiftly silenced
by fast tyres and hard steel.
Roadsides and hedgerows
littered with creature corpses

baked hard and decaying.
Offering themselves up
-as a sky burial.
Hawks circle above
to exploit the miscalculation.

Why do only some birds fly so low,
What provokes such suicidal tendencies?
Remnants of iti manu glued to tarmac
Just a few scraggly feathers erect.
A flag billowing a cautionary tale.

8

THE UNFORTUNATE FISHERMAN

A COLONY of sprawling weeds congregated on the far side of the notorious Waikato river. Shags straddled rocks that breached the murky water, drying their wings warily.

Dirty clouds of thick fog menaced the lower limbs of dying trees. There was a noticeable absence of people here too. This spot on the river was notorious. Locals knew to avoid it. It was said to be *Tapu*.

Ignoring the warnings of superstitious locals. The visiting fisherman was determined to try his luck. He fancied himself a rainbow trout. It was a rarity to find a fishing spot uncrowded.

The Fisherman stood atop the riverbank, rod in hand. Casting out his lucky spinner, aiming for the riffles behind the rocks. His back and forth motion was faultless.

Almost in a meditative state, he felt relaxed. The process of casting out and reeling in, most satisfying. His eyes fixated on the spinner's black body, its gold accents dazzling as it danced amongst the water.

The clouds conspired to veil the sun. It seemed suddenly cold and eerily quiet. Then without warning, the bank surrendered. Clumps of dirt crumbled away. His boots slipped, losing their grip. He breathed in sharply, trying to freeze momentum. He lost his stomach to foreboding.

The birds in the trees stopped their chatter. For a moment, the river held its breath.

Upon his cautious exhale, the precipice shunted the unfortunate fisherman. The shags took to the skies.

He shouldn't be here, and he knew it.

He stumbled, losing his rod as he fell. He was panicking now. Grabbing at the scrambling bank. His clawing fingernails filled with loose clay as he plummeted, gathering momentum.

His head collided with a sharp rock as he tumbled. Fresh warm blood matted in his hair. He was helpless and heading for the rabid froth of the galloping flow below.

Tethered reeds trembled as he plunged deep into the waters rampaging ire. His jersey and jeans clung heavy and sodden to his sinking frame. He bobbed and sank then bobbed, and gasped, tasting gulps of weedy water.

His eyes wide open in shock and terror. No one saw him fall. There was no one here to save him.

Disturbed sediment muddied the waters. The Fisherman was winded and confused, the river held him captive in its chaos.

He caught a glimpse of something charging up from the inky depths below. A charcoal shadow the size of a kauri log. The monster's colossal mass slammed hard against him.

The fisherman was stunned.

The *Taniwha* coiled its lengthy girth around the fisherman, who struggled wildly in defence.

Struggling for breath, fighting both the river and his own sense of disbelief. It can't possibly be a Taniwha, maybe that bang to his head had made him hallucinate. He felt his ribs crack. Taniwha aren't real, he thought to himself. They are just mythical monsters, made up to scare children. As he struggled, the Taniwha clamped down harder, squeezing the breath out from his lungs.

He flayed his limbs and tugged and pushed and pulled. He was frantic. Fighting to break free of the Taniwha strangling his torso.

Agitated water saturated his senses. It rushed in his ears and gushed up his nostrils. The weight of the Waikato filling his belly.

Glaring up through his calamity he could just make out a figure, slowing to look at the broken bank and his abandoned fishing rod. They seemed to stop and look around.

With a sense of renewed hope, he lashed about wildly trying to get their attention. Mustering what strength remained he attempted again to make the surface, desperate and dying for air. The figure on the bank picked up his fishing road and continued on, out of sight. It was futile. With no breaths left, he resigned to his fate.

With wide eyes he watched the quivering light on the surface diminish as he sank. The *Taniwha* swam back to its pulpy cache, the unfortunate fisherman snared within its unyielding grip.

9
WAS THE WATER COLD?

The old wharf's / bones
   creaked beneath bluish skies.
Running - the plank
   we leap
for the Sun
     Mid-air,
fervor *stretching*
like worn elastic.

Mountains stand vigil.
We each take turns
   tumbling
the lakes embrace.
    A ripple effect.
  Goosebumps exhilarate,
our laughing / heads
   bob the lake.
In winter, we forget
our goosebumps.

Under the mountains gaze
an old wharf / waits.
   Bluish skies reflect.
The lake smoothes its wrinkles.
It's cold embrace
   makes space,
but we aren't there.
We aren't the same.

10
THE LOCAL

It was just past dusk at high tide. I watched as a local kid, about fifteen, abandoned his old bike under the flush of the cranky wharf light.

Unsure of myself I watched from a distance. I was the new kid with a strange accent, feeling lost in a sleepy seaside town on the underside of the world. I had been here less than a week and everything seemed so strange, the slow stretching days of sunshine and endless bare feet.

I didn't imagine then that this scruffy looking boy would quickly become like family to me.

His wild brown hair was barely tamed by an ill fitting beanie. Fishing rod in hand and a lit cigarette lolling from his cheeky smile. The red ember of his cigarette traced his sprightly maneuvers. As he navigated the doddery old wharf it swayed and groaned underfoot like a drunk.

The kid was nimble, familiar with every loose plank and rusty bolt.

He could be found here on most evenings, and during the daytime too. Preferring it to the confines of a stuffy class-room, where all he seemed to get was in trouble.

His eyes scrutinized the swell and his fishing rod followed. He made his way back along the sides of the wharf. Dangling a morsel of bait amongst a school of little piper swarming the colonizing mussels.

He needed to catch a little piper. A colourful specimen sprightly enough to entice a John Dory to his line, or maybe even an elusive kingfish,

He was keenly watched by wharf visitors. Mainly holiday makers. Stragglers at the tail end of the season, there to breathe the briny air and admire the disco lights of candied boats nodding in their moorings.

Some of them noticed how he wiped his bait knife clean upon his pants. They noticed the stains on his hoodie too, and how his toe poked out from a yawning hole in his left shoe. Engrossed in his own enterprise, he remained oblivious to their concern.

The wharf's knees buckled and groaned as he jumped down to the lower platform, hauling up his first piper. He lit another cigarette, 'borrowed' from his mum's pouch.

He used his lit cigarette to burn the line whilst his hands and teeth busied themselves twinning fishing line, attaching a new rig to his rod.

He had learned about knots and rigs by watching calloused hands of old skippers. They'd taken a shine to the boy, frequently offering him scraps of bait and nuggets of hard-earned wisdom. In return he joined in their banter and on occasion helped them unload their boats. He observed them, noticing how their weathered eyes tracked seabirds working the water.

More bystanders were watching now. Some squirmed as he used the hook to pierce the piper's body. It wriggled desperately as he lowered it back into the sea.

Feeling a little braver, I had made my way out from the shadows and found myself standing beside him. He turned to acknowledge me, offering me a cheeky smile and his pouch of tobacco.

Then he waited.

Holding the tension of his line between his thumb and forefinger he stared out to sea. His concentration was unwavering. This kid knew his stuff. Prince of the wharf.

The slapping of the tide against the wharf could not disguise the rumbling in his stomach. He was hungry and in need of a meal. His mum would be in the Pub until closing.

11
THE JOKESTER

THE NICE LADY serving coffee at the market detects a slight twang of an accent when I say, "Thank you."

"That's a lovely accent Dear, where does it come from?" she asks.

I am reminded that I am a stranger. It throws me, it always throws me. I am a chameleon no more. How do I explain my presence here?

She's passing pleasantries but I feel like a fraud. The fractured accent is of obscure origin. My Loki voice is a jokester. Sliding uninvited into conversations. Suggesting to those that *really* know me that I'm either very happy, or very mad, or somewhere in between.

I don't know where I come from, not really!

I was born in a city I never once slept in. And my family of boomerangs immigrated frequently to new towns, in other countries. Some boxes were never unpacked.

My voice is a choir of cicadas on a humid night in Huntly. It had butchered Christmas carols for pennies and pounds on a housing estate in the nineties.

I've lived by the coast, near a gold mine, in a housetruck, in a tent. My toes are spread wide from a childhood in bare feet, my porcelain skin tinged olive.

I have lived.

I smile when I think of it. All the people that I have been. But you can't say all that to a stranger at a market.

I pause to think and sip my coffee, careful to prevent the froth forming a mustache on my lip.

"Everywhere," I reply with a smile. A lamington's pink and white crumbs settle like confetti on my plate.

12

THE SLUMBERING
SPIRITS SPEAK

I CAN SMELL the Glenfiddich long before I take a sip. It smells of heather in the highlands. It tastes like the aftershave of imperial stags on the prowl. Fumes rising from stout glasses advocate my intoxication.

I can see my grandad when I take a sip. See him holding his own, the gathered coterie captivated. Whisky in hand and a smoldering King Edward cigar held theatrically. He speaks, igniting the passion that bathes with warm whisky in men's bellies.

Everyone looks and nods, cheering. Spontaneously banging glass bottoms on table tops to applaud his spiel. Encouraged, the old boy continues.

He is eminently positioned. Stretching over his protruding stomach, old braces cling bravely to his favourite grey trousers.

Holding court, he exhorts the virtues of brotherhood with a genuine conviction that cannot be suppressed, he speaks of the working man's plight and the price of fish n chips. The men listen intently, their expressions smudged by the smoky haze.

It is an acquired taste, I'm told, enjoyed by a more sophisticated palette. A ten year old single malt cannot be hurried.

And so I hold it in my mouth to see if I can make myself enjoy it. See if I can train my tastebuds to become refined. I'm sure I pulled a sour face after swallowing that first nip. I hoped no one noticed. I do not like whisky. Not at all. I like vodka. But I persevere.

I swirl the whisky around and around the glass and watch it swirl. Biding my time. Gathering up the nerve to take another sip and down another mouthful. Attempting to summon remnants of my Scottish ancestry and awaken their spirits hibernating dormant in my blood and marrow.

It becomes apparent as the evening endures that my ancestors could barely recall the sweet bouquet of the wild heathers brush. They had never heard the Stags roar rattling the lowlands or grown accustomed to the taste of a single malt.

My ancestors instead haunted the smoggy filth. Their toil embedding cobbles of grimy streets. *Bairns* snatched dead from nursing mothers whose common grief languished in rows of cold houses. They wore meager rags brandishing the impermeable stench of smelting iron, industry leaching out from within their dirty pores. Smouldering factories were their landscape whilst the workhouse and gallows loomed heavy on the periphery.

There was no respite for their wretched souls except the numbness served warm at Alehouses and filthy brothels. Churches attended sporadically. Paying lip service and hedging bets on behalf of the dead, whose broken backs built empires.

At least that's how the stories were told as the whiskey flowed and I dared to ask, how did I get here and where did I come from?

13
THE WILD WITHIN

A SQUEAL PIERCES the peace at 3am. Somewhere in the house, a baby's cry. Startled, we tumble from our slumber. We have no babies here.

Instinctively we seek out the squeal. Surging adrenaline motivates our limpish limbs, already reluctant to cooperate. My little toe catches the wardrobe corner as I shuffle blindly in the dark.

Boisterous dogs wide awake. Racing claws abruptly halt, scorching through worn carpet. Two tails wagging erect, their noses down sweeping in circles. Teamwork. The cat disturbed. Marauding now on the room's perimeter.

Our eyes adjust. At the epicentre of the chaos, a baby rabbit. Sodden fur exaggerates its fragile frame.

The cat is noisy, resigned but visibly agitated. She's lost her rabbit now. Either to the dog's jaws or to our best intentions. Stalked with one eye and lugged inside a window by a mouth of broken teeth. Her prized prey is a hunting toil wasted.

The rabbit frantically seeks refuge, dashing for a tight spot behind the old fire sitting idle, awaiting winter.

A flurry of action. The lounge quickly secured. Noisy dogs barking from behind our bedroom door. The cat out of sight vocalizing its disapproval and the rabbit behind the fireplace just beyond our reach.

The 4am conversation between two middle aged adults. Husband and wife, semi naked and still half asleep

"I was standing here, did it go past you ?"
"I didn't see it go past me."
(A pause, a yawn)
"It must still be behind there."

We stare at the fireplace waiting for inspiration, while our minds navigate the stupor of our sudden rush to wake.

A fists bangs the fireplace, soot dusting our sleepy faces. Once, twice, a third bang. The dogs bark louder, their claws scratching frantically at that bedroom door.

The rabbit stays hidden.

His arm reaches behind the fireplace. The arm stretches, bending fingers flex feeling blind for damp fur hiding behind cold metal. He grabs at the rabbit. She squirms away. He grabs it again, a firmer grip and passes her to me. She sits calmly in my arms as I carry her back outside through the dark and drizzle.

Guided by the silhouette of the veteran Totara flanking the gate. I push through strands of grass. Soggy tentacles strangling my ankles as I make my way to the back paddock. I set her down and off she goes. I watch her run. Back home to her mum in the warren. I imagine that's where baby rabbits go.

Her mum will probably scold her for being so careless and nearly getting herself killed, but relieved she'll hug her baby tightly. Thankful that she made it home at all. Finally she will warn her to be far more *careful* next time. But a close call cannot always protect against the tenacity of a hunting cat. A slew of headless corpses are a brutal testament to our old cat's predatory prowess. A missing eye and broken teeth unable to repress her innately feral nature.

I am grateful that such torture wasn't a baby rabbit's fate, she's safe for tonight, at least.

He is already back in bed but not quite snoring. The dogs circle and settle. Sensing me, he lifts his arm and I snuggle into his chest. His eyes stay shut but he gasps a little when I warm my wet feet on his legs.

14
ŌTAUTAHI IN WINTER

Out West
beyond the sea,
past plains of buttered grass.
Foothills unfold
to valley roads
that wend
and crawl
tall titans.
Straddling
veiny threads
of river beds,
Mountains pose.
Crests in veils
of virgin
snow.

A whisper
grows
from craggy breath,
whipping cold
in skin
and bone.
A hawk
upon the updraft.
Steep Peaks
stretch skies
of
fading denim.
Winter jewels
in Alpine crowns.
Beyond the vista
down below.
the city shivers.

15
THE DEVIL'S KISS
TRIGGER WARNING

Spat out from deep within the prison pit and flanked by two lumbering men, I staggered through a haze of human waste and misery. Dragged through the dust and the crowd I shielded my eyes from the harsh winter's sun.

The waiting gallows came into focus.

Each hair on my neck stood erect. Enlivened by my racing heart, every thought screamed at me to run or fight or beg, anything to avoid meeting my fate at the end of that cruel short rope.

I struggled violently and broke free from my chaperones, making a dash for a gap in the crowd. The mob quickly closed ranks so I fought through them, desperately kicking and throwing fists. I was frightened yet fierce but within moments the scuffle was over and

I was recaptured. The humiliation resumed as I was paraded like a pariah back through the centre of the crowd, who threw rotten fruit and stones in retaliation.

I searched the hateful stares of those who had gathered. Former neighbors and friends. Frantic, my eyes darted between the faces, seeking any hope from an ally.

"Mary.....Mary." I pleaded to a familiar face.

Avoiding eye contact, Mary stared blankly ahead.

"Mary...I'm not a witch. I'm innocent. You know me! We've been friends for years, Mary. Mary...Mary" my voice was drowned out by the baying crowd.

Unwashed and unkempt, I was undoubtedly a terrifying spectacle as hails of spit thundered down on me.

The village atmosphere was ugly, and charged with fear. Shivers raced the length of my spine. Terrified and awash with sweat. I had never felt so utterly alone.

In my last moments I recalled the unfortunate events which had brought me before the gallows.

The breaking dawn had seen clear skies painted crimson red. Exhilarated by the crisp November air.

I had skipped home, swooning with whimsical recollections of a magical evening spent with Mark. Excited by his tales of life beyond the village and seduced by his dark eyes.

I had quietly crept in through the back door. Still happily caught up in my own secret world. I hadn't seen it coming, Master David wielding the book that knocked me senseless and off my feet.

Demonology had claimed its first blood. The smile I'd been wearing all evening slipped instantly. It would never return.

Master David towered over me. "Are you a witch?" he shouted. I felt the colour drain from my face.

Still slightly confused but sensing imminent danger, I made a run for the door but Master David's enormous frame blocked the exit. His eyes met mine and with a sinister smile he slammed the door shut and pulled the bolt locked. Launching me back across the kitchen with a sharp backhand.

"Are you a witch?" Master David repeated. Thumbing through the book he held, the questions came quickly.

"Where did you get your healing powers, Gillie, and where do you go late at night?"

He leaned down to me. A crumpled pile of a girl cowering on the cold kitchen floor.

He was armed with the instruction manual for witch hunting. Apparently penned in person by Scotland's new King James. I'd heard mutterings of witch hunts and witches amongst the villagers. Discovering a witch in your midst would certainly curry Royal favour.

Two other male figures emerged from out of the shadows. Out came the periwinkles. The interrogation began.

I could feel every slow turn of the thumbscrews. With each denial, the screws tightened just a little more. Pain like none I'd ever known seared through me.

I screamed hoarse as my flesh ripped and shredded, vomiting loudly between screaming and sobbing. I was in shock and just wanted it to stop, but the men didn't relinquish and wouldn't let up.

My torment continued. Amidst screams, my bones cracked and one by one each finger shattered at the knuckle.

Eventually, the periwinkles were removed. My mangled hand was hot and swollen.Lamenting its loss; I cradled it momentarily like a dead baby. My respite was short-lived.

Rough rope was wrapped around my face and head. The two men held the rope, an end each, ready to tighten.

Master David leaned in towards me, close enough that I could taste the ambition on his breath. Again he spat his accusations at me.

Aggravated by my repeated denials, he simply nodded to his accomplices to tighten the ropes.

I pleaded for mercy as Master David paced the floor and my head was crushed and cut.

"Confess Witch and we will stop the wrenching."

My eyelids seemed suddenly heavy, closing of their own accord and for a fleeting moment the pain subsided. I was back in the meadow with Mark and I almost felt his kiss upon my forehead.

My eyes reopened quickly as pain coursed through my body again. Blood pooled in my mouth, the overflow gurgling out from my swollen lips. Gasping for breath I tried to scream my innocence, but it was futile.

Master David thought me a witch. I would be banished from his house regardless.Live or die in this room today, I was done for.

The rope was eventually removed. I did not die and I would not confess. So on it went.

Dragged up by my hair roots, out from the bloody remnants of my wrenching.

I was pushed onto the kitchen table. Held down while cruel men's hands tore at my clothes. Ripping and pulling them from my battered flesh.

"Look for the devil's mark," Master David instructed. Absolute terror froze me. I was helpless, naked and alone. Poked and prodded. My skin crawled as strangers searched and violated my body.

"What's this.... what's this?" Master David was excited. Forcing my neck to one side, revealing a fresh love bite, or the 'mark of the witch'.

I was exposed. My secret was tainted forever. Discovering the 'witches mark' extinguished the light within that the broken bones and bloodied beatings had not.

"Stop.......Stop." I pleaded. This violation broke me.

"Are you a witch? Tell me and it stops." It was all I could do to nod in agreement.

In a daze of confusion and exhaustion, I responded to the clues I was given. I made mention of Heather, and rowan berries and how I helped the midwife Agnus.

Conjuring up a *Demonology* style narrative. Similar to the one Master David had already set on in his mind. His eyes widened with excitement.

I was a coward. In exchange for some respite from my suffering, I named names. I sentenced them all to a fate similar to my own. Their pain and suffering are a stain on my soul.

I heard whilst in prison that they all named names too. Sacrificial lambs purifying the village of its idiots and its misfits and its poor.

Stood shaking now in the shadow of the gallows. I shut my eyes against the spitting hordes. Trying to banish their slurs from my mind.

Any hope of salvation slipped away as the hangman's rope scratched over my face. I could feel my heart drumming its own funeral March.

Now balancing on that terrifying precipice of inevitability. I was determined, my final thoughts would not be of them.

I had experienced very little control over my own life. My peasantry predetermined, my job decided for me. I had lived at the whim of others, except for Mark. I had chosen Mark wholeheartedly and without reservation. My memories of him were moments of snatched happiness.

Trying to stop my knees from buckling beneath me, I could hear the gallows groan. I took deep breaths, aware that I would only have a few breaths left to take. My knees weakened again and my whole body shook. With another breath I squeezed my shut eyes tighter still and forced my mind to escape to happier times.

I was back in the meadow on that cool November evening. Surrendering to a lovers frenzy, giggling as the feathery heather tickled my bare flesh. Disheveled but satisfied, I rested my head upon Mark's chest. He gently stroked my hair as I listened to his heartbeat returning to rest.

AUTHOR'S ACCOMPANYING NOTES:

This creative nonfiction/fiction hybrid piece is based on the Scottish witch trials of Gillis Duncan.

Recognition for all those who suffered these injustices has been slow, and retelling the stories of suffering endured by these women and men is particularly relevant at this juncture. Especially in the context of an historic apology offered by the General Assembly of the Church of Scotland, who on 24 May 2022 issued a statement to "acknowledge and regret the terrible harm caused to all those who suffered from accusations and prosecutions under Scotland's historic witchcraft laws, the majority of whom were women, and apologise for the role of the Church of Scotland and the General Assembly in such historical persecution".

The Devil's Kiss stands not only as a narrative of a young woman's personal demise but as an example. It is a cautionary tale that demonstrates the devastation inflicted when church & state turn citizens against one another in pursuit of the enemy within. Fueled by hysteria, and without restraint, the power and violence in its response is unyielding. Inevitably, as a result, there are real and catastrophic consequences for societies most vulnerable and powerless.

16

BABA YAGA

Flanked by two large dogs
I walk along a country road.
The night in pursuit,
a hag at my heels.
Under her bleak coat tails,
the night hag morphs
gnarled trees into sinister silhouettes.
Her wretched face of darkness
bedeviling familiar landscapes.

I walk our regular route
roosting birds in the bushes
flutter nervously as we pass.
A cackling Morepork incisive.
The dogs startled by
thunderous hooves
of scattering sheep.
The night hag advances.
We walk on.

Loose gravel crunches underfoot,
scratching claws menacing.
Remnants of burned rubber
follow the roads curve.
Snagged in the bough
of veteran tree branches
the rising moon yawns.
Her face no longer polished sterling.
Crooked and yellow, like an old hag's teeth.

From the treetops
a Morepork cries "Baba Yaga"

17
THE JOYS AND PERILS
OF DOG WALKING

WATER SHOWERED off Dana's back as she emerged from the river, a large stick limp in her jaws. She waited for my approach. Gnawing at the stick now clamped between two paws.

I wobbled over river stones, making my way to her. Hurling the stick for a final time before wiping slobbery hands along my pants.

Dana barreled after the stick again shredding dirt underfoot. Absorbed in the pleasantries of a Sunday afternoon, Dana and I had deviated much further on our walk than ever before.

Blackberry thorns tore at my shirt as I clambered after Dana, who raced up and out of the riverbed. In quick pursuit I clawed my way up the bank on hands and knees, the crumbling dirt wedged beneath my fingernails. I emerged in an unfamiliar clearing, and dusted myself down.

A fantail sleuthed Dana as she rushed to explore the hemming bush. Her whip of a tail stood erect and her nose was fixed firmly to the ground. Captivated by a scent she rushed off again, following a trail of gouged dirt and fresh tyre tracks. I lumbered behind her. She stopped abruptly to growl at something large covered by bloodsoaked sheets, partially concealed under sparse brush.

Battling a swarm of midges I rushed to slip on Dana's leash. She stood firm, froth coating bared teeth. I hauled her back but she remained vigilant. Her chest puffed out, her stance wide and the raised hairs along her back pronounced.

I paused to look around, aware we were in remote territory. My eyes followed the deep gouges scarring the ground and trenches of muddy puddles recently displaced. A vehicle track meandered off to create a narrow path through the trees.

Gossiping magpies, aware of our presence, swooped the tree-tops. I strained to listen for other noises on the periphery and considered the possibility that maybe we weren't alone here.

Dana had calmed a little but her rumbling growl persisted. The blood seeping through those sheets seemed fresh, soaking parched ground.

I dared not imagine what lay beneath those sheets. Should we hastily retreat and hurry back to more familiar terrain? Or should I entertain my curiosity and take a proper look.

I paced back and forth before the large mass, chewing the inside of my cheek, as was my habit when nervous. Ruminating on the possibility that what lay hidden beneath the brush could possibly be a *person*.

Aware that something seen can never be unseen. I allowed my imagination to run through the gauntlet of horrific possibilities, and their nightmarish ramifications.

Those that love the missing have no peace, I thought out loud.

Despite my apprehension, I felt compelled into action.

Quietly I edged closer. I held my breath and carefully lifted the edge of the sheet with a stick. I forced myself to look as I struggled to lift the sodden sheets a little higher.

Underneath the sheets, the prickly black hair of a wild boar. At best guess, the boar appeared prepped and disemboweled for pick up by a returning hunter. I had looked longer than I needed to. Taking in the full tusks, the half-opened snout grasping onto a final breath. I instinctively covered my mouth to stop myself from vomiting.

Then stumbled backwards, almost tripping. As I dropped the stick, the makeshift shroud fell too. I was relieved it wasn't a person laying there. But still, the boar's eye blankly staring was unimaginably disturbing.

I slowly became aware of myself, aware too that Dana had resumed her frantic pacing. I'm sure I could hear barking in the distance, getting nearer.

Pig dogs.

I could just make out the rumble of a running pack gaining ground.

We quickly left the scene. I unleashed Dana and we hurried back the way we came. I plowed through bramble bushes. Stopping only to pry out stray thorns snagging my clothing, The image of the boar remained fresh in my mind. Stepping carefully over river stones, I was still shaken and shadowed by a strange sense of unease.

The river coursed away old water, as it always did. Dana found a new stick to chew. Yet I wrestled with a subtle shift in my mood. The unexpected face of death wedged itself as a splinter beneath my skin.

ACKNOWLEDGMENTS

1. Saturation: Winner of the Loud Coffee Press Annual Haiku Competition. Published in Loud Coffee Press, volume 3, Issue 1, winter 2022.
2. The Unfortunate Fisherman: First Published by Etherea Magazine Issue 14, September 2022.
3. The Rag Doll Rider: Was awarded second place prize for nonfiction and Published in cacophony by Havik: Journal of Arts and Literature, May 2023.
4. The Fable of the Spider and the Housemate: First published in ' I used to be an animal lover' anthology, May 2023.
5. The Slumbering Spirits Speak: First Published in Issue 1 Lemon Spouting May 2021. (defunct)
6. The Devil's Kiss: First Published by Remembering the Accused Witches of Scotland, August 2022.
7. The Jokester: First Published by Panorama: The Journal of Travel, Place, and Nature Issue 9.
8. Riding Mountains: First Published in erbacce journal 73, 2022.
9. Was the Water Cold? : First Published by Fieldstone Review, Issue 15 Reversals, 2023.
10. The Wild Within: First Published by Scissors and Spackle Issue 17, 2021.
11. Winter in Otautahi: Published on toiotautahi.org, 2022.

12. Baba Yaga: First Published in New Myths, September 2023.
13. Iti Manu: Published by Havik: Journal of Arts and Literature, 2020.
14. The Joys and Perils of Dog Walking : First Published by Bacopa literary Review, November 2023.

ABOUT THE
AUTHOR

Donna spent her childhood between countries. One foot bare and carefree in New Zealand, the other tiptoeing the coal dust and camaraderie of working-class England.

She lives in Rangiora, New Zealand, with 'Mr. Faulkner' but likes to roam.

Donna has been published in Erbacce, Takahē: Hua/ Manu, The Typescript, Tarot Poetry New Zealand, Fieldstone Review, Etherea Magazine, New Myths, Written Tales, and many others.

She has had both fiction and poetry published in numerous anthologies. She won the Loud Coffee Press Annual Haiku and Rune Bear Quarterly Drabble contests in 2022. She made the coveted longlist for the Erbacce Poetry Prize in both 2022 and 2023, and she was awarded second place for her nonfiction story: 'The Rag Doll Rider' by Havik in 2023. She has work forthcoming in both the Bacopa & Windward Review. You can connect with Donna on Instagram @lady_lilith_poet/Twitter @nee_miller.

https://linktr.ee/donnafaulkner

9 798223 473831